How Much Is $100.00?

Carey Molter

Consulting Editor, Monica Marx, M.A./Reading Specialist

ABDO
Publishing Company

Published by SandCastle™, an imprint of ABDO Publishing Company, 4940 Viking Drive, Edina, Minnesota 55435.

Credits
Edited by: Pam Price
Curriculum Coordinator: Nancy Tuminelly
Cover and Interior Design and Production: Mighty Media
Photo Credits: Hemera Studio, PhotoDisc, Rubberball Productions, Stockbyte

Library of Congress Cataloging-in-Publication Data

Molter, Carey, 1973-
    How much is $100.00? / Carey Molter.
        p. cm. -- (Dollars & cents)
    Includes index.
    Summary: Explains what a one hundred dollar bill is, how it compares to other dollar bills, and how many hundreds are needed to purchase different items.
    ISBN 1-57765-893-0
    1. Money--Juvenile literature. 2. Dollar, American--Juvenile literature. 3.
    Addition--Juvenile literature. [1. Money.] I. Title: How much is one hundred. II. Title.
    III. Series.
    HG221.5 .M655 2002   2002071707
    332.4'973--dc21

SandCastle™ books are created by a professional team of educators, reading specialists, and content developers around five essential components that include phonemic awareness, phonics, vocabulary, text comprehension, and fluency. All books are written, reviewed, and leveled for guided reading, early intervention reading, and Accelerated Reader® programs and designed for use in shared, guided, and independent reading and writing activities to support a balanced approach to literacy instruction.

Let Us Know

After reading the book, SandCastle would like you to tell us your stories about reading. What is your favorite page? Was there something hard that you needed help with? Share the ups and downs of learning to read. We want to hear from you! To get posted on the ABDO Publishing Company Web site, send us email at:

sandcastle@abdopub.com

SandCastle Level: Beginning

How much is
one hundred dollars?

This is a one hundred-dollar bill.

One hundred dollars **is the same as one hundred one-dollar bills.**

This is how to write one hundred dollars.

$100.00

One hundred dollars **is the same as twenty five-dollar bills.**

One hundred dollars **is the same as ten ten-dollar bills.**

One hundred dollars **is the same as five twenty-dollar bills.**

$100.00

This globe costs $100.00.

That is one one hundred-dollar bill.

$200.00

This TV costs $200.00.

That is two one hundred-dollar bills.

$300.00

This blender costs $300.00.

That is three one hundred-dollar bills.

$400.00

How many dollars does
this rug cost?

(four hundred)

21

Picture Index

globe, p. 15

one hundred dollars,
pp. 3, 7, 9, 11, 13

one hundred-dollar bill,
pp. 5, 15

rug, p. 21

More about the
One Hundred–Dollar Bill

Benjamin Franklin

All bills have the signature of the secretary of the treasury

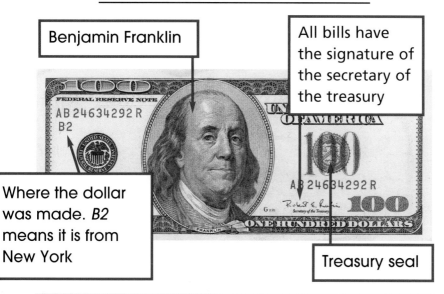

Where the dollar was made. *B2* means it is from New York

Treasury seal

Independence Hall

23

About SandCastle™

A professional team of educators, reading specialists, and content developers created the SandCastle™ series to support young readers as they develop reading skills and strategies and increase their general knowledge. The SandCastle™ series has four levels that correspond to early literacy development in young children. The levels are provided to help teachers and parents select the appropriate books for young readers.

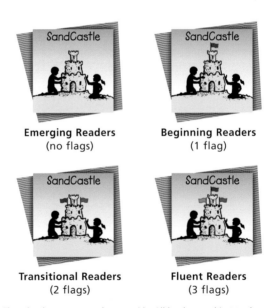

Emerging Readers
(no flags)

Beginning Readers
(1 flag)

Transitional Readers
(2 flags)

Fluent Readers
(3 flags)

These levels are meant only as a guide. All levels are subject to change.

To see a complete list of SandCastle™ books and other nonfiction titles from ABDO Publishing Company, visit **www.abdopub.com** or contact us at:

4940 Viking Drive, Edina, Minnesota 55435 • 1-800-800-1312 • fax: 1-952-831-1632